The Orchestra Musician's CD-ROM Library™

Vol. I

TIMPANI/PER

Beethoven, Schubert and more

It's Never Been Done Before

The Orchestra Musician's CD-ROM Library™ is an unprecedented collection, affording musicians the opportunity to build their own personal library of orchestral repertoire at an incredibly low price. **If these parts were purchased separately, this collection would easily cost $500.00 or more.**

The Orchestra Musician's CD-ROM Library™ can be used by virtually all computers. Works are viewable and printable on either PC or Macintosh using the CD drive of your computer. No access codes or special software is required. The CD employs Adobe Acrobat Reader which is included on the CD. Use the CD drive in your computer to view each part or to print letter-size copies with your printer. Complete system requirements are found on page 8 of this booklet.

Go to WWW.ORCHMUSICLIBRARY.COM for the latest news on upcoming volumes.

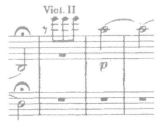

Publiée pour la première fois de cette manière. La bibliothèque CD-ROM pour des musiciens d'orchestre est une collection nouvelle qui permet aux musiciens d'orchestre de créer une bibliothèque personelle du répertoire orchestral à un prix extrèmement bas. Le CD-ROM ci-joint contient les parties imprimées de 90 chefs d'oeuvre orchestral. L'achat des parties separées de cette collection couterait au moins $500,00. Les oeuvres sont à voir et à imprimer par un PC ou ordinateur Macintosh en utilisant le lecteur CD-ROM. Ni password ni software sont de rigeur. Le CD est muni de Adobe Acrobat Reader Technology.

In dieser Form zum ersten Mal publiziert. Die CD-ROM Bibliothek für Orchestermusiker ist eine noch nie dagewesene Zusammenstellung, die es orchestermusikern zu einem unglaublich niedrigen Preis ermöglicht, sich eine eigene persönliche Bibliothek der Orchesterrepertoires anzulegen. Die beigefügte CD-ROM enthält die gedruckten Stimmen von 90 Werken der Orchestermusik. Einzeln gekauft, würden die Stimmen dieser Zusammenstellung mindestens $500,00 kosten. Ansicht und Druck der Werke mittels CD-ROM Laufwerk von PC oder Macintosh. Weder Password noch spezielle Software erforderlich. Die CD ist mit Adobe Acrobat Reader Technology ausgestattet.

Pubblicate la prima volta in questo modo. La biblioteca CD-ROM per gli orchestrali è una collezione mai realizzata che permette ai musicisti di formarsi una biblioteca propria del reperto rio orchestrale. Il CD-ROM accluso contiene le parti stampate di 90 opere per orchestra. Comprate singolarmente le parti di questa collezione ammonterebbero almeno a $500,00. Visione e stampa delle opere attraverso il lettore CD-ROM del PC oppure Macintosh. Non sono necessario né una password né un software speciale. Il cd è dotato di Adobe Acrobat Reader Technology.

Nunca se había hecho esto antes. La biblioteca CD-ROM de música orquestal es una colección sin precedentes, dándole la oportunidad a los músicos de construir su propia biblioteca orquestal a un precio increiblemente bajo. El CD-ROM contiene las versiones imprimibles de las partes de los mejores 90 trabajos orquestales. Si estas partes fueran compradas separadamente, esta colección podria costar facilmente $500.00 o mas. Estos trabajos se pueden ver e imprimir en PC o Macintosh usando el CD drive de su computadora. No son necesarios códigos de acceso o software especial. El CD se imprime con Adobe Acrobat Reader Technology el cual esta incluido en el mismo.

Copyright © 2003 by CD Sheet Music, LLC
International Copyright Secured   Made in USA   All Rights Reserved
Exclusive Distributor for USA, Canada, Australia and Japan: Hal Leonard Corporation
Exclusive Distributor for the European Union: EMS Music — Europe & America

Table of Contents

Daniel-Francois Auber
Fra Diavolo Overture

Ludwig van Beethoven
Symphony No. 1 in C Major, Op. 21
Symphony No. 2 in D Major, Op. 36
Symphony No. 3 in E♭ Major, Op. 55 "Eroica"
Symphony No. 4 in B♭ Major, Op. 60
Symphony No. 5 in C Minor, Op. 67
Symphony No. 6 in F Major, Op. 68 "Pastoral"
Symphony No. 7 in A Major, Op. 92
Symphony No. 8 in F Major, Op. 93
Symphony No. 9 in D Minor, Op. 125 "Choral"

Piano Concerto No. 1 in C Major, Op. 15
Piano Concerto No. 2 in B♭ Major, Op. 19
Piano Concerto No. 3 in C Minor, Op. 37
Piano Concerto No. 4 in G Major, Op. 58
Piano Concerto No. 5 in E♭ Major, Op. 73 "Emperor"
Violin Concerto in D Major, Op. 61
Concerto for Violin, Cello and Piano in C Major, Op. 56
        "Triple Concerto"

Ah! Perfido, Op. 65
Consecration of the House, Op. 124

Beethoven (con't)
- Coriolanus, Op. 62
- Creatures of Prometheus, Op. 43
- Egmont, Op. 84
- Fantasia in C Minor, Op. 80 "Choral Fantasy"
- Fidelio Overture, Op. 72
- Grosse Fuge in B♭ Major, Op. 133
- King Stephan (König Stephan), Op. 117
- Leonore Overture No. 1, Op. 138
- Leonore Overture No. 2, Op. 72
- Leonore Overture No. 3, Op. 72
- Mass in C Major, Op. 86
- Missa Solemnis, Op. 123
- Name Day Overture (Namensfeier), Op. 115
- Romance for Violin and Orchestra in F Major, Op. 50
- Romance for Violin and Orchestra in G Major, Op. 40
- The Ruins of Athens (Die Ruinen von Athen), Op. 113
  - Overture
  - Marcia alla turca
- Wellington's Victory, or the Battle of Vittoria (Wellingtons Sieg), Op. 91

Vincenzo Bellini
Norma Overture

Beethoven, Schubert and more

Hector Berlioz

Symphonie Fantastique, Op. 14
Funeral and Triumphal Symphony

Benvenuto Cellini Overture
Corsaire Overture

L'Enfance du Christ, Op. 25
Harold in Italy, Op. 16
La Mort de Cléopatre
Requiem, Op. 5
Roman Carnival Overture, Op. 9
Roméo et Juliette, Op. 17
Te Deum, Op. 22
Les Troyens: Royal Hunt and Storm

Luigi Cherubini

Medea Overture
Anacréon Overture

Gaetano Donizetti

Daughter of the Regiment Overture
Don Pasquale Overture

Felix Mendelssohn

Symphony No. 1 in C Minor, Op. 11
Hymn of Praise, Op. 52 (Symphony No. 2)
Symphony No. 3 in A Minor, Op. 56 "Scottish"
Symphony No. 4 in A Major, Op. 90 "Italian"
Symphony No. 5 in D Minor, Op. 107 "Reformation"

Piano Concerto No. 1 in G Minor, Op. 25
Piano Concerto No. 2 in D Minor, Op. 40
Violin Concerto in E Minor, Op. 64

Elijah
The Hebrides (Fingal's Cave) Overture
Midsummer Night's Dream
    (Overture and Incidental Music)
Ruy Blas Overture

Gioachino Rossini

The Barber of Seville Overture
La Cenerentola Overture
La Gazza Ladra Overture
L'Italiana in Algeri Overture
Semiramide Overture
Siege of Corinth Overture
The Silken Ladder Overture
William Tell Overture

Franz Schubert

Symphony No. 1 in D Major
Symphony No. 2 in B♭ Major
Symphony No. 3 in D Major
Symphony No. 4 in C Minor "Tragic"
Symphony No. 5 in B♭ Major
Symphony No. 6 in C Major
Symphony No. 8 in B Minor "Unfinished"
Symphony No. 9 in C Major

Fierrabras Overture
Rosamunde Overture

Carl Maria von Weber

Symphony No. 1 in C Major

Clarinet Concerto No. 1 in F Minor

Euryanthe Overture
Der Freischutz Overture
Invitation to the Dance (orch. Berlioz)
Oberon Overture

TIMPANI in C. G

Easy to Install and Use

The Orchestra Musician's CD-ROM Library™ installs and runs on Windows 95 and later and Macintosh 7.5 and later. Works are viewable and printable on either PC or Macintosh using the CD drive of your computer. No access codes or special software is required. This CD requires Adobe Acrobat Reader, which is included on the CD. Adobe Acrobat, Acrobat Reader, or Adobe Reader must be installed and working properly before using **The Orchestra Musician's CD-ROM Library™**. To install Acrobat, find the appropriate folder on the CD-ROM (PC or Mac) and click on the file. Most new computers come loaded with Acrobat Reader. Windows XP users are advised to use Acrobat 5.0 or later. If you would like to install the most recent version of Acrobat Reader, you can download it for free from www.adobe.com.

After Acrobat Reader is installed, insert the CD-ROM into your computer. On PCs with autorun enabled, the Table of Contents will appear on your screen (this may take 10-20 seconds on some computers, as Acrobat is also being opened). On Macs, find "Table of Contents" and click on it. If autorun is not enabled or if the Table of Contents does not appear, locate the file "vol$x$toc.pdf" (x = the volume number of the CD) on the CD and open it.

Once the Table of Contents is opened, simply click on a title to view or print all the parts for your instrument. It's that simple! There are bookmarks on the left of the screen and a list of composers on the first page of the Table of Contents to assist navigation to a section of the table of contents. Once a part file is opened, the bookmarks become shortcuts to the individual parts that may be in the work (for example, Flute 1, Flute 2, Piccolo). To go back to the Table of Contents and view another piece, click on "Return to Table of Contents" or close the file (PC: Control-W or click on the small "x" in the upper right corner. Mac: click on the box in the upper left corner). Note: on some PCs, clicking on "Return to Table of Contents" will leave the music file open. This may slow down some systems. To avoid this, close the file as above, or go to the Acrobat "Preferences" and uncheck "open cross-doc links in same document."

You can also use the "forward" and "back" buttons in Acrobat to return to previous pages. If any of the links or bookmarks do not work on your system, simply find the file "vol$x$toc.pdf" to open the Table of Contents.

The music files on this CD-ROM are full-size, high resolution scans of the original parts. They may be printed at full size (usually 9x12) on ledger-size paper. In most cases, you may also print full-size on legal-size paper (with smaller margins). To print on letter-size paper, use the "fit to page" command in the Acrobat print options.

System Requirements

Windows®: Microsoft Windows 95, 98 or ME: 10 MB RAM (16 MB recommended); on Windows NT4.0, 2000, or later: 16 MB RAM (24 MB recommended). 10 MB of available hard-disk space. Macintosh®: Apple Power Macintosh or compatible, MAC OS software version 7.5 or later: 4.5 MB of available RAM (6.5 MB recommended), 8 MB of available hard-disk space.

Consult our web site, WWW.ORCHMUSICLIBRARY.COM, for the latest news on upcoming volumes.